D1061162

Shawn
Mendes

By Robin Johnson

CRABTREE
PUBLISHING COMPANY
WWW.CRABTREEBOOKS.COM

CRABTREE
PUBLISHING COMPANY
WWW.CRABTREEBOOKS.COM

Author: Robin Johnson

Editor: Kathy Middleton

Proofreader: Lorna Notsch

Design, photo research, and prepress: Ken Wright

Print coordinator: Katherine Berti

Every effort has been made to trace copyright holders and to obtain their permission for use of copyright material. The authors and publishers would be pleased to rectify any error or omission in future editions. All the Internet addresses given in this book were correct at the time of going to press. The author and publishers regret any inconvenience caused if addresses have changed or sites have ceased to exist, but can accept no responsibility for any such changes.

Library and Archives Canada Cataloguing in Publication

Johnson, Robin (Robin R.), author
    Shawn Mendes / Robin Johnson.

(Superstars!)
Includes index.
Issued in print and electronic formats.
ISBN 978-0-7787-4830-4 (hardcover).--
ISBN 978-0-7787-4845-8 (softcover).--
ISBN 978-1-4271-2093-9 (HTML)

    1. Mendes, Shawn, 1998- --Juvenile literature. 2. Singers--Canada--Biography--Juvenile literature. I. Title. II. Series: Superstars! (St. Catharines, Ont.)

ML3930.M46J68 2018   j782.42164092   C2018-900272-7
                                                  C2018-900273-5

Library of Congress Cataloging-in-Publication Data

Names: Johnson, Robin (Robin R.) author.
Title: Shawn Mendes / Robin Johnson.
Description: New York, New York : Crabtree Publishing Company, 2018. | Series: Superstars! | Includes index.
Identifiers: LCCN 2018005811 (print) |
    LCCN 2018006381 (ebook) |
    ISBN 9781427120939 (Electronic) |
    ISBN 9780778748304 (hardcover) |
    ISBN 9780778748458 (pbk.)
Subjects: LCSH: Mendes, Shawn, 1998---Juvenile literature. | Singers--Canada--Biography--Juvenile literature.
Classification: LCC ML3930.M444 (ebook) |
    LCC ML3930.M444 J65 2018 (print) |
    DDC 782.42164092 [B] --dc23
LC record available at https://lccn.loc.gov/2018005811

Crabtree Publishing Company

www.crabtreebooks.com   1-800-387-7650

Printed in the U.S.A./052018/BG20180327

Published in Canada
Crabtree Publishing
616 Welland Ave.
St. Catharines, ON
L2M 5V6

Published in the United States
Crabtree Publishing
PMB 59051
350 Fifth Avenuc 59ᵗʰ Floor
New York, New

Published in the United Kingdom
Crabtree Publishing
Maritime House
Basin Road North, Hove

Published in Australia
Crabtree Publishing
3 Charles Street
Coburg North
VIC 3058

3 1327 00656 3845

CONTENTS

Words that are defined in the glossary are in
bold type the first time they appear in the text.

Superstar Next Door

Shawn Mendes is a super-sweet boy next door—and an international pop superstar. The Canadian charmer was discovered on social media and became an overnight sensation. Soon his own brand of catchy **acoustic** folk-pop songs hit the airwaves. Songs like "Life of the Party" and "Stitches" rocketed up the charts and showed the world that this talented teen is something big.

Shawn is a social media superstar. Today, he has more than 27 million followers on Instagram and 16 million followers on Twitter.

Shawn began posting videos online in 2013. He performed **cover** songs from popular singers—but kept his videos short and sweet. While most aspiring singers were using YouTube to get their music out to the public, Shawn posted on Vine instead. Vine was a video-sharing app that allowed users to post looping video clips that were just six seconds long. That was enough time for fans around the world to fall in love with the young musician.

❝ He Said It ❞

"I was one of those kids who was just always on the Internet, always on YouTube, so it was easy for me to do it. It's not work. It's just fun."
—Interview in *Rolling Stone*, April 2016

Shawn was only 15 when he was discovered and **signed** to a record **label**. Since then, he has cowritten and recorded a number of hit singles, including "Treat You Better," "Mercy," and "There's Nothing Holdin' Me Back." His two studio albums—*Handwritten* and *Illuminate*—have both gone **platinum**. He's opened for Taylor Swift and **headlined** three concert tours of his own, including a sold-out worldwide arena tour. Not one to sit back and relax, Shawn has also tried his hand at acting and even has his own signature cologne—all before the age of 20.

Treat You Better

Shawn Mendes rocks—but he is not a typical bad-boy rocker. In fact, he is known for being a sweet, sensitive Canadian boy. He is friendly, polite, and patient. He always wears a warm, bright smile, gives hugs and handshakes freely, and always takes time to pose for selfies with fans. Shawn shares his feelings openly, and he spreads a message of positivity on social media. He even started a global campaign to post nice notes!

"" She Said It ""

"When we go see him at his shows, we're not just seeing Shawn Mendes, superstar. We're seeing somebody that we can say that we know because he's so open and honest with us all the time. He let us into his life and let us be a part of his journey. When we go see him, we see some of that."
—A superfan from Norway who launched a Twitter account about the superstar, in *Rolling Stone*, April 2016

Shawn's Style

Shawn's style reflects his boy-next-door personality. The modest singer prefers regular, everyday clothes over flashy fashions. He usually wears skinny jeans or khakis, T-shirts, denim jackets, and sneakers. His signature look is a plaid button-up shirt. He wore one in his first video, and soon lots of fans were showing up to his concerts in plaid!

Hearts Are Gonna Break

Shawn's soulful songs, gentle personality, and effortless style are not the only reasons fans adore him. The slim, 6-foot-2-inch, brown-eyed singer is also known for his teen idol good looks. He even won the 2017 Teen Choice Award for Male Hottie! Shawn works out each morning and takes good care of himself. But the handsome star is humble about his looks. He describes himself as "a very average guy"—which makes him even more attractive to his fans!

Made in Canada

Shawn Peter Raul Mendes was born on August 8, 1998, in Toronto, Canada. He grew up in a **suburb** of a city called Pickering. He has a younger sister, Aaliyah, who was born in 2003. Shawn's mother, Karen, moved to Canada from England and works as a real estate agent. His father, Manuel, sells restaurant supplies in Toronto. Shawn's Portuguese heritage comes from his dad's side of the family. They are a close-knit family who have always supported Shawn's supersized dreams.

Shawn describes himself as the "most average kid ever." Growing up, he played hockey and soccer. He went longboarding with his friends and watched YouTube music videos after school. But Shawn was also "a bit of a showman." He belonged to his school **glee club** and took acting lessons. He once played the part of Prince Charming, of course!

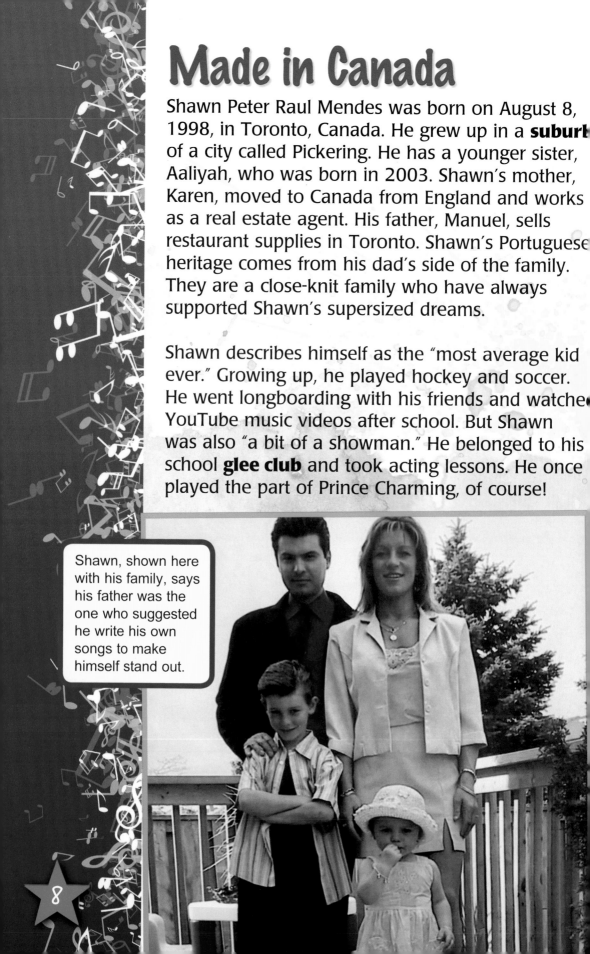

Shawn, shown here with his family, says his father was the one who suggested he write his own songs to make himself stand out.

Gone in Six Seconds

Shawn taught himself to play guitar by watching YouTube **tutorials** when he was 13 years old. He practiced playing for five hours a day. He learned songs by One Direction, Taylor Swift, Ed Sheeran, and other big artists. Then he started posting micro-videos of the songs on Vine. On July 28, 2013, he posted an acoustic version of the Justin Bieber song "As Long As You Love Me." To his great shock, the video went viral, getting 10,000 likes and followers by the next morning. Shawn Mendes had become an overnight sensation!

Princess Aaliyah

Shawn's little sister is a singer and social media star, too! She first posted videos on Vine under the name Princess Aaliyah. Today, Aaliyah Mendes has more than 625,000 followers on Instagram.

9

Meet and Greet

Within a few months, Shawn had racked up millions of views and followers on Vine, YouTube, and Instagram. His fans adored him and were eager to see him in real life. So Shawn joined the MAGCON tour that began that fall. MAGCON—which stands for Meet and Greet Convention—was a tour for popular social media personalities. He sang and played his guitar at malls and convention centers around the United States. Fans rushed to meet him and take selfies with him.

Shawn (middle) joined Nash Grier (left), Cameron Dallas (right), and other Internet stars on the MAGCON tour.

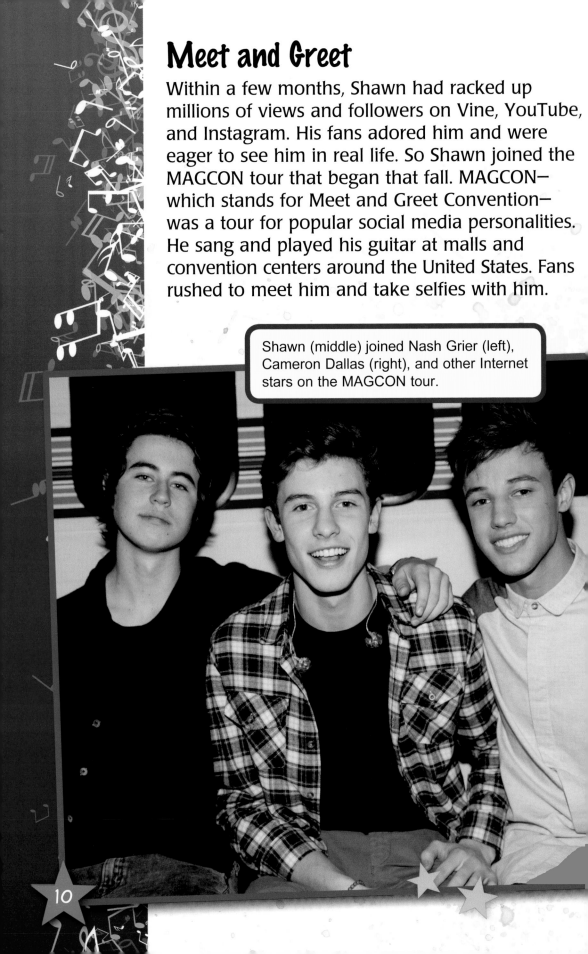

Shawn Is Discovered

In November 2013, an artist manager named Andrew Gertler saw one of Shawn's videos online. He was impressed with Shawn's natural talent—and his huge fan base. He knew right away the young performer had something special. So he flew Shawn to New York City to perform his original songs in a studio. Shawn nailed it—and landed a record deal in the process. He officially signed with Island Records in May 2014. It was the big break the social media star needed.

Andrew Gertler became Shawn's manager after convincing Shawn's parents to bring him to New York to meet with record labels.

He Said It

"I knew within the first two minutes that he's a star. It was just undeniable."
—Island Records president David Massey in *Billboard*, July 2014

Life of the Party

Shawn released his first single the next month. It was a **power ballad** called "Life of the Party" that encouraged positivity and confidence. The song was a hit, even though Island Records decided not to **promote** the song on the radio or any of the usual kinds of media. Instead, they counted on Shawn's online fan base, which had grown to a staggering 2.7 million Vine followers, to drive sales. The company's strategy worked. The single sold nearly 150,000 copies in its first week and reached the number 24 spot on the U.S. *Billboard* Hot 100. At just 15 years old, Shawn became the youngest singer to **debut** in the top 25.

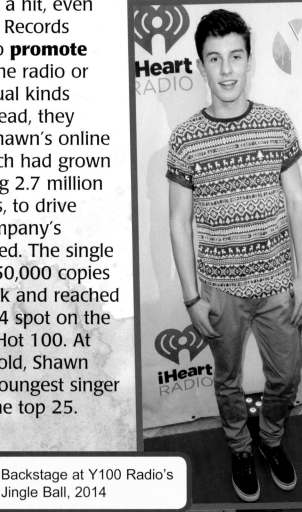

Backstage at Y100 Radio's Jingle Ball, 2014

" He Said It "

"Everything from top to bottom has happened in seven or eight months, so you rarely get time to take everything in. I keep losing myself in everything that's going on. It's so hard to take grasp of everything, but it's so phenomenal..."
—Shawn on his meteoric rise to fame, in *Teen Vogue*, June 2014

Two Tours

The next month, Shawn released a four-track record called *The Shawn Mendes EP*. The album rocketed to number one on iTunes just 37 minutes after it was released! Shawn went on the road again, opening for Austin Mahone—a singer popular on YouTube—on his North American tour. But Shawn would not be an opening act for long. In November 2014, he released his second single, "Something Big." Then he kicked off his first international headlining tour. The #ShawnsFirstHeadlines tour had seven **legs** and lasted for 10 months. It took the singer to stages all across North America and Europe. Something exciting was in the air—Shawn Mendes was on the brink of something big!

Top Dog

Shawn got his first taste of acting in 2014. He provided the voice for the main character Jake in the animated movie *Underdogs*.

Love Letters

Shawn's career was hitting all the right notes, and the super-sweet singer wanted to share the love. So he kicked off the #NotesFromShawn campaign in 2014. The social media star put pen to paper—and encouraged others to do the same. Shawn asked his fans to write short, positive messages on sticky notes and leave them on shopping carts, mailboxes, school lockers, or other places for people to find. More than 53,000 people took part and wrote nearly 260,000 notes that year. Shawn's campaign of kindness continued for another two years.

He Said It

"Every single one of you guys ROCK! Don't stop being yourself, and don't stop loving yourself for who you are!"
—A note from Shawn to young people around the world, in *Teen Vogue*, August 2015

Time and Time Again

TIME magazine named Shawn one of the 25 Most Influential Teens of 2014. And this teen was no one-hit wonder. Shawn made the list again in 2015 and 2016.

Something Big

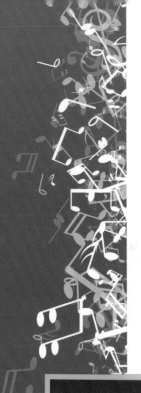

As Shawn's career continued to pick up speed, he turned his social media fame into real-world success. He released his first full-length studio album in the spring of 2015. *Handwritten* includes the songs "I Know What You Did Last Summer," "Air," and "Kid in Love," as well as his previous hit singles. The album was an instant hit. It soared to the number one spot on the U.S. *Billboard* 200 its first week! At age 16, Shawn became the youngest artist with a number one album since pop star Justin Bieber (also 16 at the time) topped the charts with *My World 2.0* in 2010.

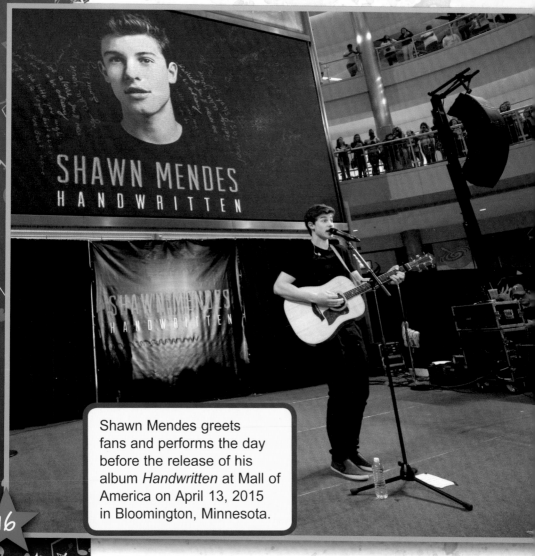

Shawn Mendes greets fans and performs the day before the release of his album *Handwritten* at Mall of America on April 13, 2015 in Bloomington, Minnesota.

Handwritten

Shawn is not just another cookie-cutter pop star. He cowrites most of his own songs. It is important to Shawn to have a voice and to create music that is true to his own experience. He has said that he wouldn't write about drugs or alcohol in his songs because he doesn't use them himself and doesn't believe using them is a good idea. He prefers to write about what he is going through in his own life. And fortunately, Shawn is finding life pretty great.

Shawn performing songs from the *Handwritten* album

He Said It

"Writing is so, so cool. It's like telling a story. When I have an opinion on something, I'm really big on making sure people hear it and what I'm trying to say."
—Shawn on writing, in *Teen Vogue*, June 2014

Breakout Hit

Shawn's third single was a **breakout** hit for the rising star. He released the song "Stitches" in May 2015. The catchy song—which Shawn says is about "feeling heartbroken and emotionally beaten up" in a relationship of any kind—really struck a chord with his fans. It topped charts all around the world and had some staying power. "Stitches" remained on the *Billboard* Hot 100 for a whopping 52 weeks! The talented teen had made the leap from the Internet to the radio.

In an interview that summer, Justin Bieber was asked what he thought of Shawn Mendes. But Justin had no idea who he was! So he checked out Shawn's music and gave him a big thumbs up!

Justin Bieber

" He Said It "

"Shawn I checked out the music and I'm so proud! So glad to see another boy from Canada crushin it. #canadiansdoitbetter"
—Justin Bieber on Instagram, September 17, 2015

Swift and Sure

People around the world began to sit up and take notice of Shawn Mendes. Pop megastar Taylor Swift handpicked him to join her **blockbuster** 1989 world tour. Shawn opened for Taylor on several stops in 2015, playing in sold-out stadiums across Canada and the United States. Calling his experience on Taylor's tour "phenomenal," Shawn said it was a great lesson for him to see that someone as successful as she is still works hard to stay on top. She also advised him not to be nervous about performing because everyone comes to a concert to have fun—not judge.

Taylor wished Shawn a special happy 18th birthday by lip-synching to "Treat You Better" in an Instagram story video.

Not the Next JB

Many people compare Shawn Mendes to Justin Bieber. Both are handsome Canadian singers who made it big at a young age. But Shawn says his music was **influenced** more by John Mayer, Bruno Mars, and Justin Timberlake. His biggest hero, though, is Ed Sheeran. Ed is a British singer, songwriter, and guitarist who Shawn describes as "a very sweet guy" and "just so normal." He may have influenced Shawn's fashion style, too— Ed often wears plaid shirts!

Shawn performing with Ed Sheeran

Shawn is a big fan of the TV sci-fi show *The 100*. He tweeted the writers to ask for a part on the show. In 2016, the show's producers gave him his wish. In his first acting role, Shawn played a minor character named Macallan, who is one of the Sky People. Macallan is caught stealing a bracelet and must perform a song to keep it. So Shawn played the piano as his character, singing "Add It Up" by Violent Femmes.

Back to School

Shawn's busy schedule made it hard for him to stay in school. He completed two years at Pine Ridge Secondary School in Pickering before leaving to pursue his music career. Shawn took courses online to earn his diploma and graduated from high school in June 2016. He had been a huge Harry Potter fan in school, carving tree branches into wands and writing his own spells. Still a fan, Shawn updated his Twitter bio when he graduated, calling himself a "Hogwarts graduate" and "full-time wizard."

Super-fan Shawn loved visiting Diagon Alley at Universal Orlando Resort in 2015. He figures the sorting hat would have put him in Gryffindor.

Looking for Love

Shawn's career has also taken a bite out of his social life. He finds it hard to date in the public eye—but that doesn't stop the rumors from flying! He's been romantically linked to Taylor Swift, actress Chloe Grace Moretz, and social media star Bethany Mota. Shawn was also rumored to be dating singer Camila Cabello, a former member of the group Fifth Harmony. The pair wrote and recorded a duet called "I Know What You Did Last Summer" and toured together in 2015. They insist that they are just good friends.

Camila Cabello calls Shawn a "charming dude."

66 He Said It 99

"The second I feel about a girl the way I feel about music is when I know."
—Interview in *Billboard*, August 2016

The Hits Keep Coming

Shawn released his second studio album in September 2016. *Illuminate* includes the singles "Treat You Better," "Mercy," and "There's Nothing Holdin' Me Back." Like Shawn's first album, it was a huge hit. It debuted at number one on the *Billboard* charts and went platinum. Shawn described the album as a mix between Ed Sheeran and John Mayer. But it is 100 percent Shawn Mendes—he cowrote every track on the album. With edgier lyrics and a more mature sound, the new album showed that the young singer was evolving as an artist. Shawn—now 18 years old—was also growing up and becoming more confident in his music and himself.

In addition to guitar, Shawn also plays piano.

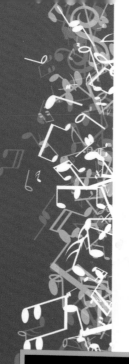

There's Nothing Holdin' Him Back

Shawn kicked off his third concert tour in April 2017, in Scotland. The *Illuminate* world tour took the singer to five continents around the globe before it wrapped up in Japan at the end of the year. It was Shawn's biggest and brightest tour yet. He performed in sold-out arenas—some packed with more than 30,000 screaming fans! When he wasn't killing it on stage, Shawn was writing and recording songs for his next album.

The *Illuminate* world tour schedule included a lot of days off, so Shawn could have fun exploring the countries he was playing.

Sweet Smell of Success

Shawn is expanding his interests beyond music, too. In 2016, he signed a contract with the modeling agency Wilhelmina. He also launched his own cologne called Shawn Mendes Signature. It is a sweet blend of rose, fruit scents, and a hint of maple to give it a "homemade, Canadian smell." The box features the star's first tattoo—a lake, trees, and Toronto's CN Tower, which together form a guitar.

Shawn walked the runway in 2017 at a show during Men's Fashion Week in Milan.

" He Said It "

"I see that my musical world has gotten so much bigger. The fact that I'm on an arena tour is insane to me. Honestly, the more things start to get bigger and better, the more I am just inspired to work harder and put my music out there and make better music and keep everything going."
—Interview in *Entertainment Weekly*, April 2017

Positively Shawn

Shawn continues to spread kindness and positivity around the world. The superstar uses his social media platform to share positive thoughts

and inspiring messages with his followers. He also raises awareness and money for **charity**. He worked with an organization called Pencils of Promise and started an online campaign called #BuildASchoolWithShawn that helped raise funds to build a school in Ghana. And he launched an online fund-raiser to help victims of an earthquake in Mexico. Shawn knows the power of superstardom and is not afraid to use it—for good.

In 2015, Shawn performed at WE Day in Toronto, a celebration to support young people in making positive change.

Shawn Mendes has found his voice—and people are singing his praises. He has been honored for his social media, singles, albums, music videos, and even his fans! He's been nominated for 10 **Juno Awards** in Canada—including Artist of the Year and Album of the Year—and he won the 2017 Fan Choice Award. He's won four Teen Choice Awards and a People's Choice Award for Favorite Breakout Artist. In 2017, he won the American Music Award for Favorite Adult Contemporary Artist—beating out his heroes Ed Sheeran and Bruno Mars for the prize!

Nice Guys Finish First

Shawn is also proud to be a **role model** for young people everywhere. Millions of fans follow his every tweet and Instagram photo. Do they see bad-boy temper tantrums, wild parties, or smashed guitars? Not even close. Shawn would rather have marathon ping-pong tournaments with his friends than party like a rock star. He is kind and polite and respectful. He stays true to himself and keeps it real with his fans—and they love him for it.

" He Said It "

"I ran head first into the industry when I was 15 and so it feels very natural for me to be honest to be this way. I like being able to be a role model for people, especially younger kids."
—Interview in *Paper*, September 2017

Anything Is Possible

So where does the superstar-next-door go from here? He is busy writing and recording songs for his next album, due in 2018. His music is growing and changing as quickly as he is, and he thinks the new record will surprise fans. Shawn also wants to try his hand again at acting. He is preparing to rock the big screen in an upcoming musical comedy film called *Summer of Love*. He'll star in the movie about a road trip that takes place in 1967, the year young people gathered in San Francisco to celebrate what became known as the Summer of Love. After that, Shawn says, "Anything is possible."

" He Said It "

"When I'm 22, I could be a completely different person, not because fame [or] my career has changed me, but because that's how life is. I could be an actor. I don't really like to say this is where I'll be in five years because I truly have no idea."

—Interview on *Larry King Now*, September 2016

Timeline

1998: Shawn Peter Raul Mendes is born on August 8 in Toronto, Canada

2013: Shawn posts his first six-second video on Vine

2013: Goes viral after posting acoustic version of the Justin Bieber song "As Long As You Love Me"

2013: Artist manager Andrew Gertler discovers Shawn when he sees one of his videos online

2014: Island Records signs Shawn

2014: Debut single, "Life of the Party," is released

2014: Shawn opens for Austin Mahone on his North American tour

2014: Release of debut record, *The Shawn Mendes EP*

2014: Shawn launches his #NotesFromShawn campaign of kindness

2014: His second single, "Something Big," is released

2014: Shawn kicks off his first international headlining tour, #ShawnsFirstHeadlines

2015: Shawn's first full-length studio album, *Handwritten*, soars to number one on the US *Billboard* 200 chart its first week

2015: His third single, "Stitches," is released.

2015: Shawn opens for Taylor Swift on her 1989 world tour

2015: Shawn's duet with Camila Cabello, "I Know What You Did Last Summer," is released

2016: Shawn appears on the season three **premiere** of the TV show *The 100*

2016: The Shawn Mendes world tour begins

2016: The song "Treat You Better" is released as the lead single from Shawn's second album

2016: Shawn graduates from high school

2016: The single "Mercy" is released

2016: His second studio album, *Illuminate*, is released

2017: The single "There's Nothing Holdin' Me Back" is released

2017: Launches a cologne—Shawn Mendes Signature

2017: Shawn wins the American Music Award for Favorite Adult Contemporary Artist

Glossary

acoustic Performed without electric instruments

blockbuster Very big and successful

breakout Suddenly and extremely popular or successful

charity An organization that provides money or other help to those in need

cover A performance or recording of a song that was previously recorded by another artist

debut To appear or to be performed in public for the first time

glee club A group of people who get together to perform songs

headline To be the main attraction or star of a show

influence To affect or shape someone's life or work in an important way

Juno Awards Annual Canadian awards for musical artists that is similar to the Grammy Awards in the U.S.

label A company issuing a brand of commercial recordings, usually under a trademarked name

leg One segment of a long concert tour

platinum Describing a record album that has sold one million copies

power ballad A slow, soft rock song with strong and emotional vocals

premiere The first public showing of a TV show, movie, or other performance

promote To share information about a product to help sell it

role model Someone who shows others how to behave well

signed Hired by a record company

suburb An area of houses on the edge of a city

tutorial A book or online lesson that teaches you how to do something by explaining each step of a process

Find Out More

Books

Caravantes, Peggy. *Shawn Mendes: Pop Star*. Momentum, 2017.

Croft, Malcolm. *Shawn Mendes: Ultimate Fan Book*. Big Buddy Biographies. Carlton Books, 2017.

Mostow Zakarin, Debra. *Shawn Mendes: It's My Time*. Scholastic Inc., 2016.

Websites

Visit the official Shawn Mendes website for music, videos, news, concert updates, and more: www.shawnmendesofficial.com/

Join the Shawn Mendes all-access fan club at this website: https://shawnaccess.com/

Social Media

Check out Shawn's posts and pictures on his Twitter feed: https://twitter.com/ShawnMendes

Visit Instagram to see the superstar's pictures and videos: https://shawnaccess.com

Index

About the Author

Robin Johnson is a freelance author and editor who
has written more than 75 children's books. When
she isn't working, Robin enjoys traveling, feeding
her sock monkey obsession, and trying to outwit
her husband and teenage sons in strategy games.

28 DAY BOOK
Hewlett-Woodmere Public Library
Hewlett, New York 11557

Business Phone 516-374-1967
Recorded Announcements 516-374-1667
Website www.hwpl.org